CW00871312

Old Edgware
In Camera

by Alf Porter

QUOTES LIMITED of BUCKINGHAM

MCMXCI

Published by Quotes Limited
Whittlebury, England in 1991
and in this second impression 1992

Typeset in Plantin by
Key Composition, Northampton, England

Pictures Lithographed by
South Midlands Lithoplates Limited, Luton, England

Printed by Busiprint Limited
Buckingham, England

Bound by Charles Letts Limited
Glasgow, Scotland

© Alfred Ernest Porter 1991

All rights reserved. No part of this publication may be reproduced,
stored in a retrieval system, or transmitted, in any form or by any
means, electronic, mechanical, photocopying, recording or
otherwise, without the prior permission of Quotes Limited.

Any copy of this book issued by the Publisher as clothbound or as a
paperback is sold subject to the condition that it shall not by way of
trade or otherwise, be lent, re-sold, hired out or otherwise circulated
without the Publisher's prior consent, in any form of binding or
cover other than that in which it is published, and without a similar
condition including this condition being imposed on a subsequent
purchaser.

ISBN 0 86023 376 6

Further reading:

Rev. B.J. Armstrong, *Some of the Parish of Little Stanmore* (Edgware, 1849)

Percy Davenport, *Old Stanmore* (Stanmore, 1933)

Charles L. Holness, *St Lawrence Church, Little Stanmore: A Short Guide* (Harrow, 1937)

Royal Commission on Historical Monuments England: Middlesex (London, 1937) pp.16-17 and 113-115

Walter W. Druett, *The Stanmores and Harrow Weald Through the Ages*, (Hillingdon, 1938)

George Cross, *Suffolk Punch*, (April, 1939)

Arthur Mee, ed., *Middlesex*, (London, 1940)

Norman G. Brett-James, *Middlesex*, (London, 1953)

Michael Robbins, *Middlesex*, (London, 1953)

C.F. Baylis, *A Short History of Edgware and the Stanmores in the Middle Ages*, (London, 1957)

Friends of Saint Johns: *A Guide to the Parish Church of Saint John the Evangelist, Great Stanmore*, (Stanmore, 1965)

R.B. Pugh ed, *Victoria County History f Middlesex*, Volume IV (London, 1971)

Peter G. Scott, *Harrow and Stanmore Railway*, (Greenhill, 1972)

Alan W. Ball, *The Countryside Lies Sleeping*, (London, 1981)

Joan Johnson, *Excellent Cassandra*, (Gloucester, 1981)
Princely Chandos, (Gloucester, 1984)

Acknowledgements are due to Stephen Castle for his help with the text, and to Pamlin Prints.

Introduction

There are still may people living in Edgware who can remember when the area was basically a farming community, when the traffic on the roads was dominated by the horse and when Edgwarebury Lane and Pipers Green Lane were what their names imply — hedge-lined country lanes, not the built-up, house-lined roads we know today, or when the village blacksmith plied his trade on the east side of the High Street. But there must be many thousands more who settled here after the tube railway came to Edgware in 1924, who must find it hard to visualise what a country area it once was.

Edgware is not mentioned in the Domesday survey but is referred to in a charter of AD987 where it is spelt *Aegceswer*. The history of the area goes back much further than this date, as excavations at Brockley Hill have revealed evidence of occupation in the Mesolithic period, c8000-4000 BC — Bronze Age flints, including an arrow head. Brockley Hill is also believed to be the site of *Sulloniacae*, a flourishing Roman pottery manufacturing centre in the 1st and 2nd centuries AD and occupation of a more domestic nature continued into the late 2nd, 3rd and 4th centuries AD.

Edgware High Street owes its prosperity to being part of the great Roman Watling Street, running from Dover, *via* London and Saint Albans, to Chester. This prosperity is illustrated in the number of inns and alehouses on this short stretch of road.

On the Edgware side there were four: namely, the Nine Pins and Bowl, the George, the Boot (at one time called the Boot and Spur) and the Leather Bottle. On the Little Stanmore side there were nine: the Load of Hay, the White Lion, the Crystal Palace, the White Hart, the Jolly Dealers, the Chandos Arms, the Masons Arms, the Sawyers Arms and the Beehive.

This may seem a lot for such a small village, but the reason is that a stage-coach horse could run from eight to ten miles before needing to be changed — the village, at eight miles from London, was ideal for the first change going north and for the last change before entering London.

FRONT COVER: Edgware crossroads viewed to the south c1880. On the left is the Boot Public House, once called the Boot and Spur. It was a popular stopping-place for carters and drovers. Opposite is the Masons Arms public house. All the shops and buildings on the east side (left) were demolished in 1930 to make way for the dual-carriageway.

Edgware High Street, view to the north in 1903; the White Lion Inn is on the left and opposite was the entrance to Bridge Farm. Note the state of the road; old records tell us that in the winter there were normally nine inches of mud and even in the summer, after rain there could be four inches.

Laying the tramway track outside the White Lion Inn in 1904.

Edgware High Street, view to the north in 1903; the west side (left) is in the Parish of Little Stanmore (Whitchurch), while the east side (right) is in the Parish of Edgware. Of the inns and ale houses, the early 18th century facade of the White Hart Public House is on the left. A water seller waits by the gas lamp.

Edgware High Street in 1920 shows the survival of large numbers of historic buildings and a tram in the distance.

The east side of the High street c1900; the gig is outside the farriers, possibly waiting for the horse to be shod. Higher up the hill to the left is the sign of the timber-framed and gabled George public house.

The village smithy, High Street, c1910; the timber-framed and jettied building, now demolished, dated from the 15th or 16th century.

Edgware High Street, view to the north in 1910. The sign of the George Inn can be plainly seen.

The High Street view to the south c1903-1905. The 15th century George Inn is on the left and the village smithy a little lower down.

The High Street, showing some of the 15th and 16th century buildings c1900-1905.

Edgware Council School; the fence down the middle of the playground was to separate the boys from the girls.

Edgware Council School group, Standards four and five, 1912.

The timber-framed George Inn in the High Street. Note the drinking trough and the rails for tethering horses, c1900.

The Chandos Arms c1905-1910, a rambling timber-framed building of the 16th century or earlier date, originally called the Crane and said to be the finest coaching inn in the district. To the right is the Old Court House where W. S. Gilbert (of Gilbert and Sullivan fame) was a magistrate.

A group of villagers, apparently a wedding scene, outside the Old Court House in the High Street c1890-1900. The carts are standing outside the timber-framed Chandos Arms.

Edgware Volunteer Fire Brigade's picture was taken in the stable yard of the Chandos Arms c1900.

W. (Bill) Newell, captain of the local fire brigade, with firemen Marsh, Gillie, Farrer and Millard.

The volunteer fire brigade with their new motor appliance c1930.

A group of children in front of Edgware Methodist Chapel c1900. This was number 63 High Street, where later Lavender's butcher's shop was built.

A group of unemployed march through Edgware, while returning to Northampton after a demonstration in London c1905.

Edgware 5 2 1904 SGA

A group of locals near the crossroads included some of the older villagers and young ladies dressed in the then height of fashion, with white aprons and fur boas. The tramway tracks are being laid in 1904.

Laying the tramway in the High Street outside the Chandos Arms in 1904.

Edgware crossroads; the sign of the Masons Arms is on the left while across the road is the Boot Inn. On the right is Station Road.

The Light Railways Order of 1901 called for a clearance of fifty feet when a tramway was being laid; as this was not available in the High Street, the fronts of the buildings opposite the Masons Arms (east side) had to be cut back, c1904.

A typical tramcar of the Metropolitan Electric Tramways Company Limited, with its open upper deck. In 1936 the trams gave way to trolley-buses, which ran until 1962, when they in turn were replaced by motor 'buses; motor 'buses had been operating on other routes from before 1914.

The old Masons Arms on the corner of the High Street and Whitchurch Lane. On the left is Prudens shop, the local saddler and harness maker, c1920.

The High Street viewed to the south in 1903. The Masons Arms sign is on the right and in the distance (centre) is the sign for the Chandos Arms.

John Chapman, the carrier, loading up outside the stables of the Boot public house.

Timber-framed houses on the west side of Edgware High Street c1910; note numbers 65-67, a timber-framed hall house dating from c1500, which survives.

The crossroads at Edgware. The Masons Arms is on the left and the Boot Public House is on the other side of the road; view to the north c1900.

The Boot Public House and the village pump (behind the railings on the right), c1903.

Edgware High Street view to the north in c1935. The rebuilt Boot Public House is on the right. It was demolished in 1965.

PC Rowe on horse-back, Edgware High Street c1905.

The Boot Public House after the fire in the stables in January 1907. They were of timber-framed construction and dated from the 16th/17th centuries.

Edgware High Street: view to the south c1930.

Tram standing in Edgware High Street at the corner of Manor Park Crescent in front of the London and South Western Bank, which was later Barclays Bank. Behind the tram is 'Blacking Bottle Lodge', at the entrance to Edgware Place, a mansion now demolished. This house was once owned by a Mr Day, who in 1828 built Day's Almshouses at Stone Grove, Edgware.

OPPOSITE: Close up of 'Blacking Bottle Lodge'. ABOVE: Edgware Post Office c1910: the gabled, timber-framed building in the centre, which dates from c1500, survives as a restaurant.

The dedication of Edgware Village War Memorial c1920.

The War Memorial, High Street, Edgware — view to the north c1935.

Edgware High Street, view to the north, before 1904: the coffee house on the left was once an alehouse called the Sawyers Arms and later the Post Office. The village war memorial was built in the space in front c1920, and the so-called Handel's smithy is to the right.

This group, possibly from the Beehive Public House, on an outing to the seaside includes J. Attmore, J. Hunt, A. Porter, G. King, P. Cornish, Wally Porter and Bill Porter.

The main entrance lodges and gates to Canons in 1904-1905; it was the seat of James Brydges (1674-1744) who became the first Duke of Chandos in 1719. The lodges and ornaments have been demolished but the gate piers have survived.

Edgware High Street view to the south in 1903: the bottom of Canons Drive is just to the right. Note the poor condition of the roadway.

The Leather Bottle public house, Stone Grove, Edgware c1913.

The Leather Bottle public house, Stone Grove c1903: on the right are the Atkinson's Almshouses, which were built in 1680, but alas rebuilt in 1957.

The Leather Bottle, Stone Grove before 1900.

Stanmore Corner (now known as Canons Corner) — view to the north in 1904; the roadway is part of the old Roman road of Watling Street.

Stanmore Corner c1930; an Automobile Association man is on traffic duty and a tram proceeds southwards.

A group at Edgware: Doctor Findlater (seated in uniform) is with his wife and daughter, and nurse Copas (on the right).

St Margaret's Parish Church, Edgware c1905; the west tower, which dates from the 15th century, is all that survives of the medieval church. The remainder was rebuilt in 1764 and enlarged in 1845. Edgware did not become a separate ecclesiastical parish until the 13th century.

St Margaret's Parish Church: interior view of the nave, chancel and aisles c1905.

LEFT: The Rector of St Margaret's Parish Church, Edgware c1890. RIGHT: The Rector's daughters c1890.

St Margaret's Churchyard, Edgware; human remains removed from the church crypt because of flooding were reinterred on 10 April 1905.

Edgware Station Approach c1895.

Steam Rail Car of the Great Northern Railway at Edgware.

Steam-hauled passenger train at Edgware Station in June 1937; the Station opened in 1867 and was the terminus of the Edgware and Highgate Railway. It was closed to passenger traffic in 1939.

Hale Lane, Edgware c1924; the gate on the left was the entrance to Edgware Rectory, now the site of a cinema, originally called the Ritz. The building on the right occupies the present Broadwalk shopping mall.

The Ritz Cinema on the corner of Station Road and Manor Park Crescent, in the 1930s.

Edgware Tube Station, Station Road in the 1930s.

Station Road, Edgware, the shopping centre in the 1930s.

Edgwarebury Lane c1920; Purcell's Avenue now runs to the left.

This typical country footpath at Edgware leads from Station Road across the stream to the Hale and Mill Hill.

The water splash in Hale Lane, c1920 — note Goff's Farm, now the site of Farm Road.

Hale Lane in the 1920s; the water splash was just over the hedge to the left.

Lower Hale Farm, (now Stonyfields Lane); a graceful early 18th century farmhouse, in the 1920s.

The Green Man public house, The Hale, Mill Hill in the 1920s.

The Hale Station, Great Northern Railway was the first stop after leaving Edgware and was close to Mill Hill Midland Station.

One of the vagrants who lived rough in the lanes and waste ground when Edgware was a country village, 1924.

W. E. Higham's Edgware tug-of-war team in 1906 included back row: PC Rowe, Tom Moore, Tom Cornwall and Bill Stonebridge; sitting: W. E. Highams and Alf Halsey.

Edgware police cricket team, c1910.

LEFT: The archway leading to the stable yard of the Chandos Arms — a drawing by Horace Wright, who was the local chemist and historian, 1924. RIGHT: These buildings in the High Street date from the 15th/16th centuries and were demolished to make way for the dual-carriageway; a drawing by Horace Wright, 1924.

LEFT: Old buildings on the west side of the High Street near the cross roads; a drawing by Horace Wright, 1925.
RIGHT: This building was at one time an alehouse called the Sawyers Arms; a drawing by Horace Wright, 1924.

LEFT: The interior of the George public house in 1925; a drawing by Horace Wright. RIGHT: The tower of St Margaret's Church, Edgware, 1925; a drawing by Horace Wright.

The players in a charity football match at Edgware, the Top Hats versus the Bonnets, c1920.

Some ladies from Edgware pose before leaving for an outing in the 1930s.

Index to Illustrations